Moving Monsters

Lynn Huggins-Cooper

A & C Black • London

Published 2007 by A & C Black Publishers Limited
38 Soho Square, London W1D 3HB
www.acblack.com

Hardback ISBN: 978-0-7136-7109-4
Paperback ISBN: 978-0-7136-7687-7

Editor: Sarah Gay
Designer: Miranda Snow

The author and publishers would like to thank Clare Benson and Sue Dutson for
their advice in producing this series of books.

A CIP catalogue record for this book is available from the British Library.

This book is produced using paper that is made from wood grown in managed,
sustainable forests. It is natural, renewable and recyclable. The logging and
manufacturing processes conform to the environmental regulations of the country
of origin.

Printed and bound in Singapore by Tien Wah Press (PTE) Limited.

The author and publishers would like to thank Theo Jansen for his kind permission
to reproduce the photograph on page 9.

Picture credits: front cover(br),17, Corbis Sygma; front cover(bl), Ritu Manoj
Jethani/Shutterstock; back cover, 13, Henry Diltz/Corbis; 4, Robert & Linda Mostyn;
Eye Ubiquitous/Corbis; 5, Claudia Goepperl/Getty; 6(t), Jennie Woodcock;
Reflections Photolibrary/Corbis; 6(b), D. Hurst / Alamy; 7(t), Randy Faris/Corbis;
7(bl), Alley Cat Productions/Brand X/Corbis; 7(br), image100/Corbis; 8, Photos
12/Alamy; 9, 25, Theo Jansen/loek van der Klis; 10, 24, Chris Jackson/Staff/Getty;
11, Close Murray/Corbis Sygma; 12, Getty Images/Handout; 14, Gene Blevins/LA
Daily News/Corbis; 16, Jay Dickman/Corbis; 18, Vikki Martin/Alamy; 19, Gideon
Mendel/Corbis; 20(tl), Richard T. Nowitz; 20(tr), Owen Franken/Corbis; 20(bl),
Sam Forencich/Veer/Corbis; 20(br), JG Photography/Alamy; 21(tl), Dave
Benett/Contributor/Getty; 21(tr), Adam Woolfitt/Corbis; 21(bl), Christian
Darkin/Science Photo Library; 21(br), imagebroker/Alamy; 22, David A.
Northcott/Corbis; 23, 24, Macduff Everton/Corbis

Contents

Words printed in **bold** can be found in the glossary.

Air power

We use air in lots of ways every day, to make things move or to change their shape or size.

We use it to blow up the tyres on a bike, or to blow up a mattress for a camping trip. When you blow up a balloon with a pump, you are pushing air into the balloon to make it stretch.

At a party, you might blow through a party blower to make it uncurl and make a funny noise.

FACT!

Anything that uses air to work is pneumatic. 'Pneuma' means 'air' in Greek.

Air power can also be used to make machines work. The **pneumatic** drills that dig up roads use air. The air is squashed by **pistons** that work like bicycle pumps to move a huge chisel up and down, which chips away the surface of the road.

◄ Pneumatic drills are strong enough to break up pavements and drill rocks.

Pulling upwards sucks air into the pump, and pushing down pushes the air into the ball. ►

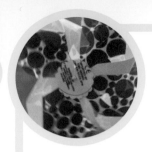

Toys that move

There are lots of toys that work by using air power. Air can make a toy jump, shake, spin, shoot, make a noise, and all sorts of other things.

▲ A toy windmill needs air to make it turn.

When someone sits on a whoopee cushion, lots of air is pushed out of the small hole and it makes a rude noise! ▶

Toy guns at the fair shoot out air to hit their targets.

Dog toys squeak when air is squeezed out of them.

You blow into a party blower to make it pop out and make a sound.

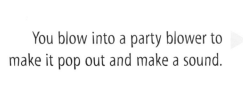

Moving monsters

> **FACT!**
> Pneumatics help to bring model monsters to life!

Air pressure has been used to make all kinds of monsters move and scare people! Model monsters in museums, in films, on television and in theme parks everywhere are powered by pneumatics.

The most famous moving monsters are in films. Even now that many special effects are created by computers, pneumatics still play a big part in making monsters move.

Models of dinosaurs, dragons, sharks, sea monsters and even vampires have been powered by pneumatics. Monsters can walk, jump, flip or scuttle with the aid of air power.

The Whomping Willow in *Harry Potter and the Prisoner of Azkaban* was built around a huge pneumatic arm to make it 'whomp' and try to hit people whenever they came near.

◀ The model alien monster in the film *E.T.* was partly controlled with pneumatics.

Try it out!

MAKE A TOY MONSTER THAT STICKS ITS TONGUE OUT

You could use all sorts of things. Here are some ideas: **a box with a flap lid (a tea box, for example), sticky tape, a straw, a balloon, card scraps, paints, coloured paper**

1 Draw a **design** on paper. It does not have to be a great drawing. It just helps you to think about how your ideas are going to work.

2 Think about how you are going to make the mouth of your monster open. How can air power make its tongue stick out?

An artist from Holland ▶ called Theo Jansen makes huge pneumatic monsters out of yellow plastic tubes. Wind blows through the tubes to make them walk, powered only by the air. This monster is called *Strandbeest*, which means 'Beach Beast'.

Breathing dinosaurs

We can see dinosaurs walk the earth once again, stomping and roaring, thanks to air power! Pneumatics are used to bring dinosaurs to life in amazing ways.

The Natural History museum in London has some lifelike models of dinosaurs in its displays. The Tyrannosaurus rex model breathes, blinks and roars at visitors. It has a **microprocessor** inside which causes the air in the valves to make the 'muscles' move.

Dinosaur monsters in the films *Jurassic Park* and *Gargantua* also moved using pneumatics. The models in *Gargantua* were controlled by a joystick. The joystick made valves in the model open and close, which allowed air to move through certain parts of the dinosaur's body. The air pressed **flexible** 'muscles', which made them move.

◄ The T. rex at the Natural History Museum has sensors so it knows where people are.

In this scene from Jurassic Park, the pneumatic T. rex peers hungrily into a car. ►

Try it out!

MAKE A BREATHING DINOSAUR!

You will need: an A3 sheet of card, a balloon, plastic tubing, a large syringe or squeezy bottle, scissors, rubber band

1 Fold the card in half. Draw and cut out a dinosaur shape, where the fold of the card is the back of your dinosaur. Open up the card to show the two sides of your dinosaur, and decorate it.

2 Cut a small hole in the fold of the card. Put the balloon between the two sides of your dinosaur and thread the neck of the balloon back through the hole.

3 Poke the end of the tubing carefully into the open end of the balloon, and wrap the elastic band around the neck of the balloon to make sure it stays attached to the tube.

4 Attach the **syringe** or squeezy bottle to the free end of the tubing. Move the plunger of the syringe in and out (or squeeze the bottle) to make the dinosaur breathe.

11

Shark attack!

Sharks are monsters of the sea, with cold eyes and teeth like daggers. The terrifyingly realistic star of the film *Jaws* is a model of a great white shark, which was powered by pneumatics.

Jaws was seven and a half metres long and needed to be able to jump out of the water, destroy a boat and 'eat' people. Inside the shark was a mass of nuts, bolts and steel. Over 150 metres of plastic tubing, 25 **remote-controlled** valves and 20 electric and pneumatic hoses made the shark move.

The boat that was attacked by the shark was also sunk and raised again using pneumatics. Barrels were attached to the boat, and when they were filled with water, the boat sank beneath the surface. When they were filled with air, the boat floated again.

◄ These huge teeth make Jaws a terrifying movie monster.

Try it out!

MAKE A MODEL SHARK THAT RISES AND SINKS IN WATER
JUST LIKE THE MODEL IN *JAWS*!

You will need: a plastic washing up bottle, a white plastic tub (an ice cream tub is good), plastic tubing, permanent marker pens, PVA glue, scissors, masking tape

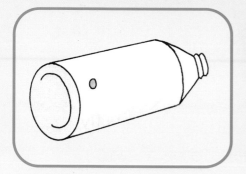

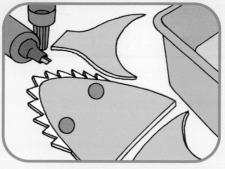

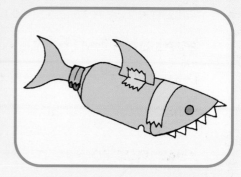

1 Cut a hole in the bottom of the bottle. This is where water will leave the model as air enters the bottle and allows the shark to rise. This will be the 'head' end of the shark.

2 Cut pieces from the white tub to make the shark's tail, fin and head. Colour them in with the permanent marker pens. Do not forget to make a line of pointed teeth!

3 Stick the pieces to the model with PVA glue – this will dry waterproof. While the model is drying, use masking tape to hold the pieces in place. You can remove these afterwards.

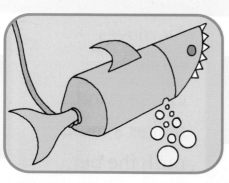

The pneumatic model shark from *Jaws* is still used for a theme park ride at Universal Studios

4 Insert the plastic tube into the neck of the bottle. As you blow into the tubing, water is forced out of the model shark by the air (your breath), and it rises to the surface. You may need to stick a small weight to the bottom of your model to stop it rolling over.

13

Halloween haunts

Halloween is a great time for making monster models! In the United States, haunted houses containing models that move and moan are created for people to visit and get a scare!

Compressed air is used to make doors spring open and ghosts fly in the air. The air makes a hissing noise as it escapes, and this adds to the spooky effect.

Carl Chetta is a talented effects inventor who creates a Halloween haunted house for visitors every year. Using pneumatics he created a trick rubbish bin called 'The Can'. Air moves through a cylinder and makes a monster push the bin lid up to give visitors a fright!

◀ Many Americans turn their homes into haunted houses at Halloween.

Try it out!

MAKE A MONSTER HAND THAT REACHES OUT OF A BIN
TO GRAB SOMETHING... OR SOMEONE!

You will need: a cardboard tube, paint, some craft paper, a party blower, a bendy straw, masking tape, scissors, glue.

1 Paint the cardboard tube to look like a bin.

2 Draw a monster arm with a scary hand at the end and cut it out. The hand should be small enough to fit inside the tube.

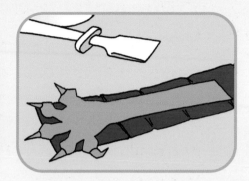

3 Stretch out the party blower and glue the arm onto it. You might need to cut a bit off the end of the party blower if it's too long.

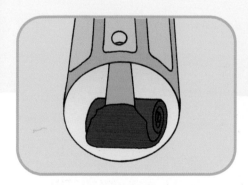

4 Cut a hole the size of the party blower's mouthpiece near the bottom of the tube. Place the blower inside the tube so that the mouthpiece points towards the hole and when stretched out the hand points towards the top of the bin.

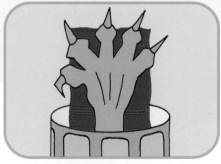

5 Push the mouthpiece through the hole and attach the straw. Blow through the straw and watch the hand pop out to grab someone!

Try to think of ways that you could make your monster hand look even scarier. Could you make it furry or stick on some horrible nails? Think carefully about how any changes you make would affect how well the device will work.

Theme parks

Theme parks use pneumatics in lots of ways. Many of the entrance gates to the rides are opened using pneumatics.

Next time you go on a ride listen for a hiss and tell your parents that it is controlled by pneumatics – they will be impressed!

Pneumatics are often used to help safety harnesses keep you securely held in place on theme park rides. Pneumatic brakes help to bring rollercoasters to a stop at the end of a ride.

At Universal Studios in Florida, a 30 foot model of King Kong used to attack one of the rides and blow banana breath all over the riders!

Pneumatic cylinders powered King Kong, who roared and picked up the train full of people before throwing it to the ground.

◀ Pneumatics ensure that safety harnesses are held securely in place.

The King Kong ride was called 'Kongfrontation' and was open from 1990 to 2002. ▶

Robots rule!

Robots are mostly built to do jobs for humans, but are also made for toys and used as characters in books, movies and television shows. They often use pneumatics to move.

Movies often show robots as monsters taking over the world and treating humans – the people who made them – very badly. This may be because people are afraid of how fast technology is developing and how robots are becoming very clever.

Robots are used in factories and workplaces to carry out work that would be too difficult or boring for people to do. Today, most cars are built completely by robots!

Robots are also used to make computers because the electronics inside are too tiny to be made by hand. People make robots for fun, too.

◄ This robot walks by using air power to make its legs move.

These pneumatic robot arms are ►
making cars in Beijing, China.

Monsters everywhere!

Monsters can be scary or cute, loveable or horrible, scaly or furry. Most monsters are fictional, but there are some real life monsters. Some monsters are a mystery, and people wonder whether they are real or not.

▲ This demon scares away evil spirits outside a temple in Vietnam.

▲ Monsters called gargoyles can often be found on old church buildings.

▲ The Loch Ness Monster is one of the most famous monsters in the world, but nobody knows whether it is real or not.

▲ Ghosts and ghouls can be some of the scariest monsters. Do you believe in ghosts?

The film Monsters, Inc. was full of friendly monsters.

A small village in Germany parades a dragon through the streets each year to remember the story of a dragon slaying.

Giant squid were once thought to be make-believe monsters. They live in the very deepest parts of the ocean and can grow to around thirteen metres long!

Trolls are said to be ugly, human-like monsters.

Bringing models to life

Model monsters can look very real and scary. Model makers use all sorts of materials and methods to bring their monsters to life. They need to think about the colour, shape and texture their monsters should be to make them look lifelike.

Monster creators often look at real life animals to get ideas for how a monster should look when they are sketching and designing their monster. They look at how real muscles work and move to help make their monster look as though it is alive.

Latex is used in film making, museums and theme parks to make lifelike moving monsters. It is a type of rubber that can be poured into moulds and then painted to make it look like skin or scales. It is very flexible, so the model can be moved into different positions.

◀ Looking at the way real animals move can help you to make your monster's movements look real.

Try it out!

MAKE YOUR MODEL MONSTER LOOK REAL!

▼ These scary monster masks are made from latex to make them seem lifelike.

1 Have a go at designing a monster using photos of real creatures or **observations** of pets to help you make it look real. Watching animal documentaries will also help you.

2 Concentrate on the muscle shapes of the animals, and watch how they walk, eat and breathe. Getting used to observing things closely will make you a better designer.

Make your own...

DESIGN AND MAKE YOUR OWN SCARY MOVING MONSTER

When drawing the design of your monster, remember it doesn't have to be a work of art! You are just putting your thoughts down on paper. Make notes around your drawing to show how you are going to join parts, and how the parts are supposed to work.

Before you start drawing, think about what you want your monster to do:

Will its mouth open?

Will it have moving wings that flap?

Will it breathe?

Will it stick its tongue out?

Will it have big googly eyes that pop out on stalks?

Think about the material you will use to make your monster – what properties will it need to have? Does it need to be flexible or can it be **rigid**?

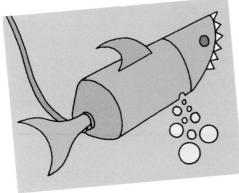

Once you have finished your drawing, show it to a friend. Tell them about how your monster will work. If you cannot explain something, or your friend asks questions you cannot answer, you may have to go 'back to the drawing board' and do some more thinking. Don't expect things to work perfectly first time. Think about how they might work better.

When you are satisfied with your design, have a go at making your model. Be prepared to stop at any point and think 'This part doesn't work.' Think about the problem and adapt your idea until it does work.

Then **evaluate** your work. Show a group of friends your finished model and explain how it works. Tell them if there's anything you would do differently next time to make things easier or to make it work better.

Brilliant books and wonderful websites

There are lots of great books and websites to help you learn more about pneumatics and monsters! When you are using the Internet, never give out details of your age or where you live, and make sure your parents and carers have a look at the websites you are visiting. They may learn something too!

BOOKS

The Knowledge: Spectacular Special Effects by Diana Kimpton (Scholastic, 2002)

Rocket Science: 50 Flying, Floating, Flipping, Spinning Gadgets Kids Create Themselves by Jim Wiese, (John Wiley & Sons Inc, 1995)

Roller Coaster Science: Wet, Wacky, Wild, Dizzy Experiments About Things Kids Like Best by Jim Wiese (John Wiley & Sons Inc, 1994)

The Way Things Work by David Macaulay and Neil Ardley (Dorling Kindersley, 2004)

Physics: 50 Great Science Experiments and Projects by Chris Oxlade (Southwater, 2004)

Dotty Inventions: And Some Real Ones Too by Roger McGough (Frances Lincoln Ltd, 2005)

The Oxford Children's A-Z of Technology by Robin Kerrod (Oxford University Press, 2004)

WEBSITES

www.the-making-place.co.uk
A great site, with lots of suggestions for things to make. You and your class can even have a real visit!

http://school.discovery.com/networks/junkyardwars
Some wonderful robots and models to make

www.usfirst.org/robotics/
For Inspiration and Recognition of Science and Technology sites

www.uspto.gov/go/kids/halloween
United States Patents and Trademarks – kid's pages of wacky inventions

www.zoonzone.com
Join Dr. Zoon on his technology quests

www.mos.org/exhibits/robot
Museum of Science – design your own robot

Glossary

compressed air	a large amount of air pressed into a small space
cylinder	a tube shape with two equally-sized circular ends
evaluate	look at something carefully to think about how well it has worked
flexible	bendable; does not break and go back to its normal shape when it is bent
latex	a rubbery, stretchy material that retains its shape
microprocessor	a circuit that controls a computer
observations	what is learnt from looking at or watching something
piston	part of a machine that slides up and down inside a cylinder to make the machine work
pneumatic	something that uses air to make it work
remote-controlled	something that is controlled from a distance using a separate device
rigid	stiff; not easily bendable
sensor	a device that responds to certain changes around it, such a movement, sound, light or temperature
syringe	a tube with a plunger used to push air or liquid into something
valve	something used to stop and start the flow of air or liquid into something by opening and closing

Index

Numbers in **bold** denote a picture.